CW00347045

TALL SHIPS ON THE TYNE

Dick Keys and Ken Smith

Tyne Bridge Publishing

Acknowledgements
Many thanks to the staff of Newcastle Libraries Local
Studies, Tyne & Wear Archives, Tyne & Wear Museums,
South Shields Library Local Studies, Kirkcaldy Museum &
Art Gallery, R.F. Gillie, Derek Henderson.

Many thanks to printers Elanders Hindson for their support.

Photographs are reproduced from the collections of
Newcastle Libraries & Information Service unless otherwise
indicated.

ISBN: 1 85795 137 9

© Dick Keys, Ken Smith, 2005

Published by
City of Newcastle upon Tyne
Education & Libraries Directorate
Newcastle Libraries, Information & Lifelong Learning Service
Tyne Bridge Publishing
2005

www.tynebridgepublishing.co.uk

Printed by Elanders Hindson, North Tyneside

Front cover: *Seascape* by Bernard Benedict Hemy c.1880-
1910. A steam paddle tug tows a ship down the Tyne. In the
background is the naval training ship *Wellesley*, stationed at
North Shields. Reproduced courtesy of Tyne & Wear
Museums.

Back cover: the masts and rigging of a collier brig on the
Tyne c.1880.

This page: Mainmast showing royal and topgallant yards,
Statsraad Lehmkuhl, Newcastle Quayside, 1987 (R.E. Keys).

Dick Keys is the author of *A Dictionary of Tyne Sailing
Ships*.

Also by Dick Keys and Ken Smith:
Black Diamonds by Sea
Down Elswick Slipways
Ferry Tales: Tyne-Norway Voyages 1864-2000
From Walker to the World
Steamers at the Staiths

By Ken Smith
Lost Shipyards of the Tyne (with Ron French)
Mauretania Pride of the Tyne
Swan Hunter: the Pride and the Tears (with Ian Rae)
Turbinia: Charles Parsons and his Ocean Greyhound

Contents

FOR THE CAPE OF GOOD HOPE,
THE fast-sailing A. 1. Barque, ACHILLES, 288 Tons Register, J. PERCHARD, Commander; will clear in Ten or Twelve Days, and has Room for Goods, and excellent Accommodation for Passengers. For Freight or Passage, apply to
CARR & CO. Brokers.
25, Broad Chare, Newcastle-upon-Tyne, 21st May, 1846.

FOR LEGHORN,
THE fine fast-sailing Coppered Brig WILLIAM PITT, DAVID BRUCE, Master, is now on the Berth for the above Port; has Room for some Light and Heavy Goods, and will be early despatched. For Particulars, apply to CARGILL, HEADLAM, & CO.
Newcastle, May 21, 1846. Quayside.

FOR BOMBAY,
WITH IMMEDIATE DISPATCH,
THE splendid fast-sailing Barque Currency, A.1. Twelve Years; H. M. WAINWRIGHT, Commander; has Room for a few Tons of Light Goods, and excellent Accommodation for Passengers. For Freight or Passage, apply to
J. WEATHERLEY, 4, Sandhill.

From the Newcastle Journal, 1846.

Two sailing cargo ships (barques) lying off North Shields ferry landing, c 1900. Ahead of them, left, lies the stationary training ship Wellesley. Passengers are seated in the small paddle ferry.

Crossing the Bar

In the middle years of the 19th century there were often over 1,500 merchant sailing ships registered in the port of Tyne. They ranged from humble coastal sloops, manned by a couple of men and a boy, to lordly full-rigged Indiamen, run with all the panache of a crack warship.

Between these two extremes were a host of brigs and barques, snows and schooners, few exceeding 400 tons. Unpretentious craft, they wandered the world looking for profitable freights. Wherever the wind blew, the sea lapped and trade beckoned, there was sure to be a Tyne-owned wind-jammer hovering in the offing.

More often than not their outward cargo was coal – the Tyne's most important export. 'Black diamonds' had for centuries been the foundation stone of the North-East economy, won from the earth by the region's hard-working miners. The sailing ships carried the coal away to destinations worldwide, with London featuring prominently as a market for this dusty mineral from the Tyne.

With sailing ships coming and going all the time, the early and mid-19th century Tyne was a crowded, bustling river. Shields Harbour must have been particularly lively – a place full of colour and movement as countless vessels of many varieties came and went, loaded and discharged. And there would be many noises – the clank of windlasses, the rattle of rope through blocks, the loud slatting of wind-caught sails, the broad Geordie shouts, the oaths of keelmen and pilots intermingling with orders being given in many unfamiliar dialects and foreign tongues.

Crews always spoke of 'Shields Harbour', including both North and South Shields in this description, since sailing vessels were moored on both sides of the river. Sometimes the harbour and the lower reaches of the river would be more crowded than usual. When a prolonged spell of easterly winds blew, combined with dangerous seas running on the Tyne Bar, ships became trapped in the river for long periods of time.

For example, in mid-December 1856 there were 727 vessels lying moored between Whitehill Point and the Low Lights, North Shields. Others lay at different points in the river. There was a total of around 1,000 ships – an avenue of masts and yards leading from Newcastle to the sea. Their average size was about 200 tons.

They were the floating homes of 7,000-8,000 seamen. Considering they were prevented from leaving the river by the adverse winds they were remarkably well-behaved seamen by all accounts. Cases brought before the North Shields magistrates were fewer than usual.

When at last the wind did become favourable and the depth of water on the bar allowed, the great fleet of sailing ships slipped their moorings and made for the open sea – 500 of them on one afternoon in early April 1857.

Perhaps the largest congregation of sail ever to be

trapped in the Tyne occurred in the winter of 1847-48 when on 4 January it was estimated that there were 1,700 ships in Shields Harbour. Six days later, 400 of this immense fleet were able to leave the river. Many had been windbound for several weeks.

The mid-19th century Tyne from which this great fleet emanated was not the deep-flowing, well regulated river we know today with its entrance protected by two immense piers. Instead, it was a sluggish, wreck-strewn, shoal-studded waterway; difficult to get out of and dangerous to get into. But for all its faults the Tyne was alive – alive with its own ships and those of other British ports and other nations. They lay moored in lines or 'tiers', sometimes seven or eight abreast.

Many ships coming to the Tyne to load coal were reported as entering the river 'light' or 'in ballast'. The terms mean the same. Both indicate that no cargo was being carried. Ballast is necessary, in the absence of cargo, to give a vessel stability. Vessels returning from the London coal voyages frequently carried shingle or chalk as ballast. But sand and other materials were also used.

Over the centuries, great hills of this imported material grew along both banks of the Tyne, often occupying valuable land. Old maps show substantial ballast hills near Bill Point at Walker, at Willington Quay, at Hebburn, Jarrow and North and South Shields. The enormous Newcastle Corporation Ballast Hill at Willington Quay generated sufficient pressure to distort the adjoining quay wall, forcing it into the river at a number of points.

Ships were charged fees to unload their ballast. By the early 1820s the going rate for this was about 20 pence per ton handled. To avoid such expenditure some owners and masters resorted to the dangerous expedient of discharging ballast before entering harbour.

For example, in 1849 the snow Marys, belonging to Alexander Scott of North Shields, was 'casting' her ballast off Souter Point, about three miles south of the Tyne entrance, when a strong westerly wind suddenly blew up. Slipping her anchor the Marys was driven helplessly before it, out into the North Sea. The wind increased to gale force.

When she was 130 miles off land her masts came down. Eventually, the crew managed to get an emergency rig together and then a providential shift of wind enabled them to get into Middlesbrough on the Tees. From there a tug brought the Marys to the Tyne – eight days after she had disappeared.

James Young's brig Gallant was not so lucky. Like the Marys she was also casting her ballast off Souter Point when a sudden squall struck her. Forced on to her beam ends, she filled with water and went down. Fortunately, there was no loss of life.

Thomas Morrison, a ballast keelman for 39 years, in giving evidence before an inquiry for the Tyne Conservancy Bill in 1849, confirmed that the practice of ships casting their ballast at sea was extensive. He went on to describe a racket, conducted by some ballast keelmen: 'Foreign vessels usually brought their ballast into the river, where the master, by means of an interpreter, entered into an agreement with the ballast keelmen to convey all the ballast away for a certain sum, that sum being near the sum it would cost to take the ballast to a regular wharf and land it.'

He explained that the keel (small barge) might be capable of taking 70 tons of ballast or more and would remain alongside until the vessel was completely emptied. However, the keel would receive barely 20 tons and the remainder would be thrown into the river. Indeed, one estimate suggests that some 20 per cent of all imported ballast ended up in the river. Small wonder the Tyne was in danger of silting up.

Charts and maps of the river published in the mid-1800s show the Tyne as something of a nautical obstacle course. Sandbanks and shoals abounded.

The first of these hazards was the Tyne Bar. This was a ridge of sand and shingle stretching across the river's entrance. The average depths of

Sailing vessels ride the turbulent seas on Tynemouth bar in this engraving based on a drawing by J.W. Carmichael, c.1820. The bar was a notorious hazard for shipping. On the right can be seen Tynemouth headland with the Priory ruins and lighthouse.

water over the bar varied between about 21 feet at high-water to 6 feet at low-water at spring tides (or just after a full moon when the rise and fall of water was at its greatest). These were optimum levels. Depths changed significantly at other times in the lunar month, or when influenced by the state of the sea or the strength and direction of the wind.

In September 1846 the water level was so low the treacherous Priors Rock became uncovered and dry. Two river pilots were able to walk across the bar. On the same day a steamer,

drawing only three or four feet of water, grounded on it, as did several light, inward-bound colliers.

The next obstacles after the bar were the treacherous Black Middens Rocks off Tynemouth (where many ships came to grief), the Herd Sand at South Shields (another major hazard for vessels), and then the Insand, which lay immediately beyond the Narrows. Even during spring tides, the depth of water over the Insand was only between eight and 18 feet. Navigating past was a tricky exercise.

It set the pattern for the rest of the run upstream. After the Insand came Durtwick (or Dortwick) Sand, then Whitehill Point Sand, Howdon Sand, Cock Raw Sand (where the river bends at Hebburn), Walker Sand, St Anthony's Point Sand, St Peter's Sand, and so into Newcastle, where ships lay aground at the quayside during low tide. At certain states of the tide the river was fordable at Newcastle. All these obstructions combined to impede the flow of water.

Further upstream navigation of the Tyne for masted vessels ceased at the low-arched 18th century stone bridge which linked Newcastle to Gateshead. This is where the Swing Bridge is sited today.

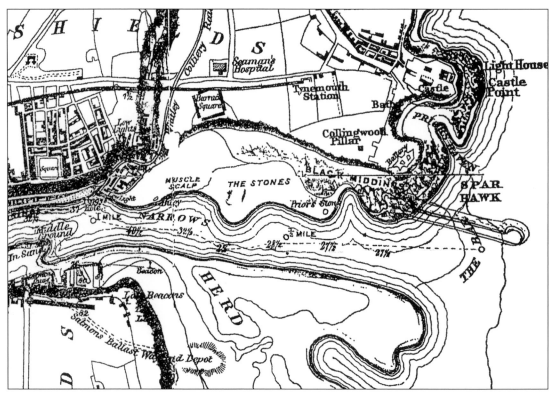

The mouth of the Tyne, showing the treacherous rocks and sands that were so hazardous.

The Tyne Bar was the scene of dramatic and tragic incidents. A strong easterly gale and a heavy sea could transform the bar into a raging maelstrom. Spectators would gather to watch vessels running the gauntlet of trying to reach the safety of Shields Harbour.

Such conditions prevailed on 5 January 1841 when a sloop was seen running towards the river. An awestruck crowd watched as she unhesitatingly ran into the welter of foam and spray which marked the bar. They gasped with astonishment when she emerged from it into the shelter of

Shields Harbour. This skilfully managed vessel was the *Newcastle & Berwick Packet*, inward bound from Kincardine. She was the only vessel to enter the Tyne that day.

However, not all ships were so fortunate. During December 1870 the North-East coast was hit by a spell of particularly severe weather. On the evening of the 8th a gale came screaming in from the south-east, bringing with it a tremendous sea and heavy rain. Dawn the following day found the steamer *Eagle* in difficulties on the bar.

A topsail schooner leaving the Tyne, 1920s or 1930s. The vessel is still under tow from a steam tug. The South Pier lighthouse is glimpsed behind.

She had developed a leak when off Whitby. With the wind behind her she had run for the Tyne. Struck by a heavy sea, her stoke hold was flooded and the fires extinguished. Another sea crashed on board which nearly sank her. Luckily, the *Eagle* came on to the Herd Sand from where her 17 crewmen were rescued by the lifeboat *Tyne*.

The stranding of the *Eagle* was followed by the South Shields barque *City of Bristol* going ashore at the north end of the Long Sands, Tynemouth. She had broken her back after striking a rock on her way in. Soon afterwards the Norwegian schooner *Amalie* came crashing ashore nearby.

But worse was to come. By the afternoon, the wind had backed to east-south-east, blowing force 10. At dusk, a schooner was sighted scudding towards the bar flying signals of distress. Struggling in the frenzied water, she had almost made it into the harbour when a tremendous sea struck her amidships. Rolling on to her beam ends, she disappeared from sight, never to reappear. For a few brief moments a body was seen floating on the surface, then just the raging sea.

In time the sea gave up evidence of its terrible power. First to drift ashore was the body of a 14-year-old boy, lashed to a spar. Soon afterwards the severed foot of a child was found. The vessel's keel floated on to rocks at Tynemouth.

Remarkably, her still legible official log was retrieved from the breakers. A vital document, it confirmed the identity of the ill-fated schooner as the *Samuel Bernard*, of Boston, Lincolnshire, and John Thrush as her master. She had been on passage from the Humber and had begun leaking. Almost certainly because of the leak a fatal decision had been made to run into the Tyne.

The full tragedy was soon revealed. Among the ship captains visiting the Tyne was one who knew the *Samuel Bernard* and her master quite well. He said that Captain Thrush usually carried his wife and five children with him. They had all been lost.

This tragedy happened despite the passing of the River Tyne Improvement Act in 1850 and the commencement of dredging operations on the bar in 1863. It was an immense task, but after many years of work the treacherous ridge of sand and shingle was removed. By 1879, the depth of water on the bar was about 22 feet at low tide.

This was by no means the only improvement made to navigation. Many of the other sandbanks and shoals in the river were dredged away, creating a deep water channel from east of the bar to Ryton. In addition, obstructive bluffs at Bill Point, Friars Goose and Whitehill Point were also removed.

The two great protective stone piers which shelter the mouth of the Tyne offer a wonderful harbour of refuge. Work began on the North Pier at Tynemouth in 1854 but it was beset with problems, being breached by storms in 1867 and again, more seriously, in 1897. The structure was therefore redesigned so that it would be straight, rather than curved. The pier was finally completed in 1909. The longer, curved, South Pier at South Shields was begun in 1854 and finished in 1895.

But few Tyne-owned sailing ships survived to use the 'new' river. Their numbers had declined as the Tyne improved. By the time the two impressive piers were completed the days of the sailing ships were nearly over and steam power reigned supreme on the seas.

Tynemouth Pier c.1890. In the distance a paddle tug tows a trading ketch into the river.

Ships and Cargoes

Coal dominated the outward bound shipping routes from the Tyne, but general cargo and passengers were also carried to numerous destinations. The coastal routes to London and other ports of the United Kingdom as well as to destinations on the near Continent were particularly important.

Colliers remained for centuries the most familiar craft entering and leaving the river. For example, on 9 January 1830, the *Newcastle Courant* reported that one vessel had 'cleared coastwise', meaning a coastal voyage, during the previous week for London with general goods. The report added, almost as an afterthought, 'also 72 colliers'. The carrying of coal by sea from the river was so commonplace that it was regarded as meriting little comment.

The report set the pattern for the rest of the year. In all, 148 vessels cleared coastwise with goods other than coal during 1830, while 11,226 colliers carried away from the Tyne more than two million tons of coal.

In the late 18th and early 19th centuries many of the vessels engaged in the coal trade to London and other destinations were brigs, snows and schooners. Snows, a slight vari-

R.E. Keys Collection

The steel three-masted topsail schooner, Alembic, built in 1894 by William Dobson & Co., Newcastle. Unlike the Alembic, most of the Tyne-owned schooners were two-masted. They were frequently used in the coal trade.

An evocative picture of sailing ships moored in the Tyne c.1900.

ant of the brig, were particularly numerous. Between 1830 and the end of the sailing ship era approximately 1,450 snows, 875 brigs, 145 brigantines and 455 schooners were owned on Tyneside. Many more ships owned and registered at other ports also called to collect the precious 'black diamonds'.

The round trip from the Tyne to London and back, which included the passage time each way, the time spent discharging coal and taking aboard ballast, usually occupied about one month, but was sometimes much longer. Colliers could be held up in the Thames for many weeks if winds were unfavourable.

However, from the 1850s onwards the steam collier began gradually to supersede the sailing vessel as the main carrier of coal. A steam collier could deliver its cargo to its intended destination with a regularity and speed which the sailing collier could not match, dependent as it was on the vagaries of the weather.

Many of the sailing vessels in the coal trade were Tyne-owned. One was the Tyne snow *Corinthian*, built in 1824 by John Laing and Sons at South Shields. It is recorded that on 14 June 1831, she arrived off Gravesend in the Thames with 344 tons of coal on board. She was just one of 223 colliers to enter the Thames within the previous fortnight, most from the North-East coast.

There was a 16-day delay before her cargo was sold, after which her master would probably have received orders for her to proceed to a buoy further up river where the coal would have been 'jumped out' by gangs of coal-whippers and transferred to barges for delivery to various wharfs and creeks on the Thames.

Coal-whipping was a method of unloading whereby the cargo was rapidly lifted from the hold in baskets using the combined weight of four men who jumped from a raised platform, each clasping an individual rope leading to a single line or runner, to which a basket of coal was attached.

By 6 July all the *Corinthian*'s cargo had been discharged – 22 days after arrival. The *Corinthian* would almost certainly have returned to the Tyne loaded with ballast to provide her with stability.

The record for the fastest round voyage from the Tyne to London and back by a sailing collier must surely go to the brig *Hilda*. Under the command of John Firbank, of South Shields, who was also the ship's owner, she left the Tyne on 7 December 1862, and arrived back in the river seven days later. It was an exceptional performance. The *Hilda* had discharged 399 tons of coal at the Regent's Canal and taken in 70 tons of ballast for the homeward trip.

As well as London, coal was carried to other ports around the United Kingdom and to ports on the near Continent. 'Black diamonds' were delivered from the Tyne to destinations including Rouen, Hamburg, Bremen, Altona, Cuxhaven, Texel, Rotterdam and Antwerp. The voyage to Rouen involved navigating some 90 miles up the River Seine.

Hamburg in particular was a port much visited by the sailing colliers and much liked by their crews. In 1814 a Hamburg company informed shippers on Tyneside they had been granted land at the mouth of the harbour for a coal wharf where the cargo could be efficiently discharged. Previously the colliers had discharged into lighters.

Much less numerous than the sailing colliers were the goods traders or 'packets' as they were sometimes called.

The barque Vesta, from an illustration in Smith's Dock Monthly. This Finnish-built vessel was owned by Harry Smith Edwards, of the High Dock, South Shields. Many years later the site of the High Dock was absorbed by Readhead's shipyard. The Vesta had a splendid reputation for rapid passage making.

These were the clippers (fast ships) of the coast. As well as general cargo these vessels also carried passengers.

They were the only sailing ships which ran, or at least were advertised to run, to some form of timetable. In the early and mid 19th century vessels left the Tyne for London every Saturday and Sunday, to Hull about every 10th day, and weekly to Berwick, Dundee, Gainsborough, Glasgow, Ipswich and many other destinations. Regular sailings were also made to the near Continent, including Rotterdam and Hamburg.

Berthing mainly at Newcastle Quay (now known as the Quayside), the goods and passenger traders must have been very well known to the general public. For the most part they were brigs, snows, sloops and schooners. The largest were on the London, Liverpool and near Continental runs. Some of the smaller vessels voyaged regularly to Gainsborough in Lincolnshire, which involved sailing 20 miles up the River Trent.

These general traders were managed by firms, families and individuals who were variously described as agents, brokers and wharfingers – Matthew Hall, Paul Ormston, John Robson, Thomas Robson, Edmund Graham, Clarke & Dunn, Joseph Shield and Nichol, Ludlow & Company were the most prominent. Some of these people owned a vessel outright, but more commonly they held a few shares in a number of vessels.

For the most part the regular traders to London were Tyne-owned and registered, as were a number running to Hull, Rotterdam and Hamburg. With schedules to keep, merchants wanting quick dispatch of their goods and passengers anxious to reach their destinations speedily in comfort, the goods trades called for vessels of excellent sailing qualities and superior fittings.

For example, Clarke & Dunn's snows *Benwell* and *Elswick* were both launched on the Tyne in 1830 especially for the London goods trade. On the morning of 5 December 1848 the *Elswick* arrived off the Tyne Bar at the end of a splendid 32-hour passage from the Thames under the command of a Captain Solomon Caroline. This was a particularly fast time.

Tyne ships also ventured regularly to the Baltic Sea ports. Every year, as soon as the ice began to disappear from the Baltic, a great procession of vessels carrying coal would set out from the Tyne and other ports of North-East England bound for this sea of Northern Europe. As well as black diamonds their cargoes might also include coke, tar, grindstones, chemicals and manufactured goods. The homeward cargo was often Baltic timber of various kinds, as well as grain, tallow and hemp. The timber was frequently destined for use as pit props in the mines of North-East England.

In May 1864 it was estimated there were between 50 and 60 ships from the Tyne, Wear and Tees lying at Kronstadt – the old Russian naval base near St Petersburg. Their crews numbered between 500 and 600 men. Such figures prompted a correspondent writing in the *Newcastle Journal* to remark: 'The Tyne and Wear burr will din the poor Russians.'

One of the hazards of the Baltic trade was a sudden 'freeze-up' which trapped vessels in their loading or discharging ports for anything up to five months. When ice threatened their departure frantic efforts would be made to get clear. In December 1835 some 20 ships became icebound at St Petersburg.

Work immediately began to cut a canal through the ice. Many men were employed. Ships began to move on the 18th of the month. It was hoped that within a couple of days they would all get clear, but a week or so later it was reported they were still frozen in. Amongst them was the Newcastle snow *Lady Cremorne*.

Sailing ships from the Tyne also carried coal and other

Sail mixes with steam at Newcastle Quay, c.1900. A topsail schooner and a brigantine (centre) with coastal steamers.

cargoes across the world's oceans, voyaging to ports throughout the globe. For example, for much of the 19th century Tyne vessels were prominent in the North Atlantic timber trade. This involved carrying timber from the east coast of Canada and the United States to ports in North-East England and elsewhere in Britain.

It was a largely summer season trade for those ships loading at ports in Canada which were icebound in winter. Given a bit of luck, a ship could be expected to complete about two round voyages to Quebec and back to Britain in the course of a season.

The six-months, ten days performance of the Newcastle full-rigged ship *Lady Westmorland* during 1868 was considered a very good one. This vessel left the Tyne on 27 March and reached Quebec by late May. After loading her timber, she came across to Greenock in 24 days. This voyage was followed by a return passage to Quebec and from there to Dundee, which was reached on 12 October after a 28-day run.

Another important trading area for Tyne-owned vessels was Portugal, Spain and the Mediterranean. Once the Napoleonic wars were over, the import of citrus fruits into the United Kingdom had developed rapidly. So far as the Tyne was concerned it was mainly oranges and the early direct import of this fruit usually formed part of a general cargo. Later, ships began to specialise in this trade. Tyne-owned vessels invariably sailed deeply laden with coal for the outward passage.

Fruit had to be landed in good condition. This called for small ships, able to load and discharge rapidly, with a good turn of speed. The schooner *Racoon* was described as a 'Newcastle fruit clipper'. She was probably the best known, and the fastest in the Lisbon orange trade.

For more than a decade this small vessel regularly brought cargoes of oranges from Lisbon to the Tyne, mainly under the command of Captain James Mundy. Typically, the *Racoon* arrived in the river on 2 January 1859 at the end of a 13-day passage with 1,037 boxes of oranges, 70 firkins of grease butter and a quantity of salt. The round voyage had only taken six weeks.

Other cargoes were also brought home by the Mediterranean traders. A number of ships were termed 'Sou' Spainers'. These vessels mainly carried coal and coke to the ports of southern Spain and Portugal, returning with cargoes of sulphur, lead and iron ore. It was a trade which grew hand-in-hand with Tyneside's developing chemical, smelting and metal-based industries. Imports seem to have begun in the late 1840s and soon southern Spanish ports became very well known to Tyne seafarers.

It was also quite common for homeward bound ships to top up with a load of esparto grass at these ports. This grass was used in the manufacture of paper. By the 1860s it had become so important that a warehouse had been specially built at Tyne Dock for its reception. In the first quarter of 1862 it was reported that seven Tyne Sou' Spainers had arrived in the river with cargoes of sulphur ore, pyrites, lead bars, copper and iron ore. Two of these, the *Britannia* and *Trenton*, had topped up with 585 tons of esparto grass between them.

Esparto grass, however, could be a hazardous cargo. At least two Tyne-owned vessels are known to have been lost due to fire starting in the grass.

One of these was the South Shields-owned full-rigged ship *Mary Spencer*. On 2 April, 1886, she sailed from Aquilas with a cargo of esparto bound for Tayport, near Dundee. Eighteen days later smoke was seen coming from pipes aboard the vessel. Large casks were filled with water and emptied where the seat of the blaze was thought to be. The hatches were kept closed. At midnight a hole was cut in the deck, a hose put through, and water pumped into the hold, but by day break it was obvious the fire was gaining.

Preparations were made to abandon ship. Attempts to get below to obtain some food were made impossible by the intense heat. The deck had become so hot that men could barely stand on it. At 5pm the Dutch barque *Marie Antoinette* was sighted, about six miles away. Seeing that help was at hand, the crew took to the boats.

Shortly before leaving, one of the men incautiously opened a hatch for just a few inches. Flames shot out, scorching his face. The fire began spreading further. Almost imme-diately after the boats were clear of the ship the main mast collapsed. So ended the career of the *Mary Spencer*, a Tyne-owned Sou' Spainer.

Sailing ships lie in the Tyne between Gateshead and Newcastle. The spire of All Saints Church near Newcastle Quay can be seen on the right, with the High Level Bridge in the background c.1890.

Last of the Whalers

For nearly 100 years Tyne sailing ships ventured into the Arctic waters of Baffin Bay and the Davis Strait on the western side of Greenland in search of whales. None of these vessels were more than 110ft in length.

It began in 1752 when the Newcastle Whale Fishing Company fitted out the *Swallow* for a voyage to Greenland. Her return, after catching four whales, was greeted with 'great joy' and the ringing of church bells. Over the years the industry had enjoyed its peaks and bemoaned its troughs. Whale stocks dwindled and revived. In 1788 the Tyne whaling fleet numbered 20 ships. By 1830 there were only four making regular expeditions to the Davis Strait and nearby waters – the *Cove*, *Lady Jane*, *Lord Gambier* and *Grenville Bay*.

The largest and most modern of these was the *Lord Gambier*, built on the River Wear. She was nearly 106ft long and almost 30ft in the beam. The *Lord Gambier* was immensely strong to cope with the buffeting and nipping of ice. Extra planking, probably up to three inches thick, was fitted over the outside planking from about half way up the hull to the keel.

In addition, there were what were described as 'ice fortifications both within and without'. At the bow these 'fortifications' are likely to have consisted of solid wood framing stretching back from the stem some 18ft.

Kirkcaldy Museum and Art Gallery

The Tyne whaler Lord Gambier, c.1860, a full-rigged ship. This is the only photograph known to exist of a Tyne-owned sailing whaler. The Lord Gambier was built in 1826 at Monkwearmouth, Sunderland, for Newcastle owners. She was lost in the Davis Strait in 1862.

Dangers of the Greenland whale fishery, engraved by W. & D. Lizars, Edinburgh, c.1810. Whaling was a hazardous occupation as this picture vividly illustrates.

The *Lord Gambier* was a three-masted full-rigged ship. Beneath her fore yard was slung a Bentinck boom. This boom was characteristic of a whaler's rig. It gave them ease of handling with a small number of men which was very useful when manoeuvring amongst the ice when most of the crew were away, in the boats, hunting whales. She was square-sterned, black hulled, with white painted ports.

Viewed at a distance, her calling would be betrayed by the distinctive, heavy wooden boat davits ranged along her sides from which her whale boats would have hung, ready for launching. The *Lord Gambier* probably carried seven or eight such boats. About 25 or 26ft long, they were manned by half a dozen or more men, including a harpooner and a boat steerer.

It was from these boats that the whales were caught, killed and towed back alongside the whaler for 'cutting in' – the gory process of butchering the whale for its oil, blubber, bone and other saleable portions. The whale species most frequently caught by the Tyne vessels was the Greenland Right Whale.

By 1830 the whalers usually left the Tyne for the Northern Fishery in late March and early April. Quite frequently a call was made at Stromness in the Orkney Islands to recruit more men and top up stores. From there a course would be set to the westward, along the 58th parallel of latitude, giving Cape Farewell at the southern tip of Greenland a wide berth because of the heavy drift ice which was likely to be encountered there.

Eventually, a course was set northwards into the Davis Strait between Canada and Greenland. It was a course often strewn with huge icebergs and veiled by darkness and fog.

These hazards were particularly lethal when combined with the storms so common to the region.

It was on the edge of the Arctic pack ice that the Greenland Right Whale was most likely to be found. Knowing this, the whalers would skirt the pack, generally heading in a northerly direction.

The 1832 hunting season was regarded as a particularly good one. The *Lady Jane* arrived back at Shields having caught 28 whales (290 tons of oil), the *Cove* came in with a tally of 37 (250 tons of oil) and the *Lord Gambier* was reported to be 'almost full'. The 1838 season was also excellent as far as the hunters were concerned. The *Lady Jane* returned safely to the Tyne after catching 23 whales, the *Grenville Bay* 24 and the *Lord Gambier* 26.

However, the 1835 season proved a disastrous one for British whaling with the loss of five ships, although none were from the Tyne. But the full-rigged ship *Lady Jane* nearly became a casualty. Trapped in the ice in 69 degrees 20 minutes North on 9 October, she remained beset with ice for over four months. The *Grenville Bay* was trapped with her for a time, but on 13 December she managed to get free.

Only a ship's length had separated the *Lady Jane* from clear water, but the same wind which released the *Grenville Bay* drove the *Lady Jane* further into the ice. Soon after, her supply of firewood became exhausted. All loose wood and stakes were burnt. Crewmen's clothing began to deteriorate and fall apart.

Thankfully, the *Lady Jane* was one of the best provisioned whalers. She was able to provide the Berwick whaler *Norfolk* with four barrels of pork. For a while 53 survivors from the wrecked Hull whaler *Mary Frances* were accommo-

The Lady Jane at sea. She was lost in the ice while on a whaling voyage in 1849.

dated aboard and fed until room could be found for them on other trapped ships.

After drifting for 1,250 miles the *Lady Jane* eventually got clear of the ice on the night of 18 February 1836. She had been badly damaged and was also leaking.

Worse still was the condition of her surviving crew members, which included 12 survivors from the *Mary Frances* who had remained on board. Most men were confined to their bunks and over 20 of the crew died from scurvy. Others were barely able to crawl.

The fittest man on board was her master, Captain John Laesk. He was the only one able to go aloft on the stormy 23-day passage from the ice pack to Stromness which was made under reefed top-sails. For the last five days of the run Captain Laesk was at the wheel almost continuously, only being relieved for brief intervals by the more able men who had to sit in chairs while steering.

Including some who passed away after arrival at Stromness, the death toll on the *Lady Jane* totalled 27 men. Among them were six Shields men. Fifteen new men were taken on board at Stromness to get the *Lady Jane* home. The ship arrived in the Tyne on 26 March after a 12-day passage.

Drawn by R.E. Keys

Last of the Tyne sailing whalers, the Lady Jane. In this drawing her rig can be clearly seen. She is a full-rigged ship and carries distinctive whaling boats on davits.

Of her original 52-man crew, only eight returned with the ship. They included Captain Laesk and the doctor, James Williamson, a young North Shields man. The remaining survivors were recuperating in the Orkneys.

By 1845 the *Lady Jane* was the sole Tyne whaler. The year 1849 saw her leave the river in March on her final voyage. She was under the command of Captain John Patterson. However, very little 'fishing' was done by her or any of the other British whalers due to heavy seas and frequent gales.

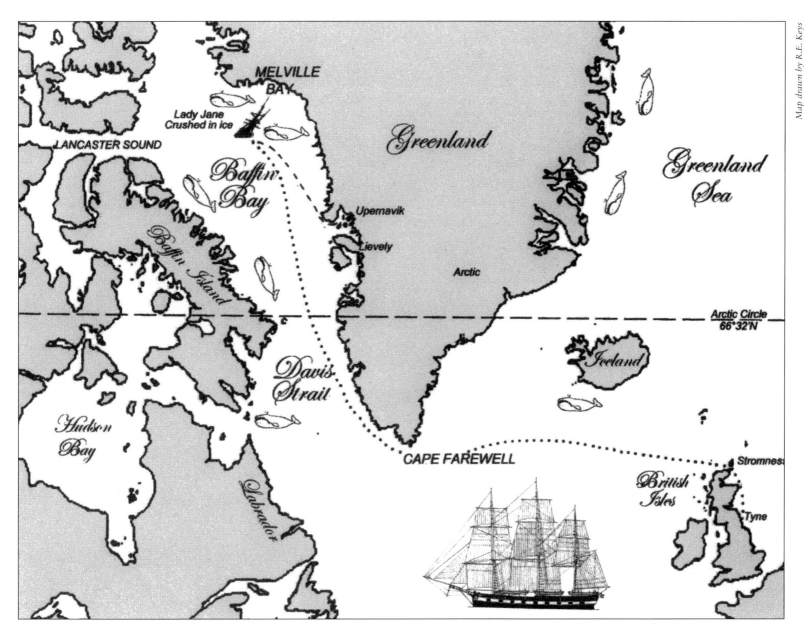

Map drawn by R.E. Keys

MELVILLE BAY

Lady Jane Crushed in ice

LANCASTER SOUND

Baffin Bay

Baffin Island

Greenland

Greenland Sea

Upernavik

Lievely

Arctic

Arctic Circle
66°32'N

Davis Strait

Iceland

Hudson Bay

Labrador

CAPE FAREWELL

Stromness

British Isles

Tyne

Adventurous voyages. The dotted line shows the track of the Lady Jane on her final voyage in 1849. The shorter line, of dashes, indicates the route taken by the men in her boats after the ship was abandoned.

On 12 June, while in Melville Bay, Greenland, in the company of eight other vessels, a great mass of ice descended on them. The first to be crushed was the *Superior* of Peterhead. Then it was the *Lady Jane*'s. turn The ice cut her in two. Her masts were brought down and within a couple of hours nothing was left to mark her ice-topped grave.

The *Lady Jane*'s 50-strong crew managed to get clear before the ship went under. They had loaded provisions and clothing into the boats. At first, along with the crew of the *Superior*, they went to the aid of the nipped New England whaler *McLeleon* whose crew were trying to save their ship. By 16 June it became obvious that the *McLeleon* was going to share the *Lady Jane*'s fate. After gathering up provisions, Captain Patterson and his men managed to launch the *Lady Jane*'s boats from the ice into the sea.

They then sailed northwards along the edge of the ice. Sometimes their route was obstructed by huge fields of ice. The boats had to be manhandled over these to regain clear water. On the morning of the 17th they made land, despite a dense fog. They now halted for a short rest and then set sail again with the aim of making for the Danish settlement of Upernavik in Greenland. Using oars and sometimes sails they made their way southwards, taking care to keep the land within their sight. They reached Upernavik without mishap.

Leaving two boats and their crews at Upernavik, Captain Patterson set out with the remaining five for Levely, another Danish settlement. They reached there on 29 June and were received with much hospitality and kindness. After a long delay, a Danish vessel took them to the Orkneys, from where Captain Patterson took a steamer to Leith and then to Shields where he arrived on 30 September. Ten others were picked up by the *Eggots Minde* of Copenhagen and 12 by a vessel named the *Gods Thaab*. These vessels landed them at Lerwick in the Shetlands on 31 October.

The escape of the *Lady Jane*'s crew had been a remarkable one, but the days of the Tyne's sailing whalers were finally over. Also at an end was the 40-year long whaling career of the *Lady Jane*.

A artist's dramatic impression of Arctic whaling.

Hazards of Seafaring

The sea of the sailing ship was a very dangerous place. In 1789 the collier *Adventure* was driven on to the Herd Sand at South Shields by a strong gale. The ship was only a few hundred yards from the beach but the sea was so rough South Shields boatmen were unable to attempt a rescue. Most of the *Adventure*'s crew were lost.

A crowd of local people gathered on the shore, helpless to intervene because of that fateful few hundred yards of raging sea. Some of the unfortunate crewmen clung to the rigging but then fell into the waves.

The tragedy which befell the ship and other vessels at the mouth of the Tyne led to the development at South Shields of the first purpose-built lifeboat, *The Original*. This oar-pulled vessel saved several hundred lives during her along career between 1790 and 1830.

Other early lifeboats based at the mouth of the river, such as the *Northumberland* and *Tyne*, also did sterling work in what was clearly a much-needed service for seamen in peril. Shipwreck was an all too common occurrence along the East Coast, with colliers, not surprisingly, featuring prominently in the toll of accidents.

The crew of a Tynemouth lifeboat, possibly the Forester No 2, pose for this picture in their oar-pulled vessel. The Forester No 2 was one of three lifeboats called out during the operation to rescue the crew of the barque Salween in 1895, but their services on this occasion were not required.

For example, in early April 1799 a fierce storm raged in the North Sea and the colliers on passage along the East Coast suffered many casualties, both in terms of ships and men. Within three days before the storm 200 vessels had departed from Shields and Sunderland, most of which had to face the full power of the wind and sea. Soon reports were coming in of ships being driven ashore, often with fatal consequences.

Among the ships wrecked in this way were the *Elizabeth*, of North Shields, which was lost near Whitburn with all hands; the *Auspicious*, and another vessel from Sunderland, which were wrecked off Newbiggin in Northumberland with several of their crew members reported drowned; and the *Ranger* of Scarborough, lost with all hands on only her fifth voyage.

Besides the *Auspicious*, no less than 12 other ships were said to have been wrecked between Blyth and Holy Island on the Northumberland coast. They were the *John*, of South Shields, one crewman saved; the *George and Mary* of Sunderland, lost on Cresswell Sands with all hands except the captain; the *Active* of Sunderland, all hands lost; the *Friends*, of Blakeney, a boy reported drowned; the *Mayflower*, of Kings Lynn, crew saved; the *Joseph and Mary*, of Newcastle, several crewmen drowned; the *Thetis*, of North Shields, crew lost; the *Charming Harriet*, of South Shields, five saved, six drowned; the *Elizabeth and Margaret*, of North Shields, crew drowned; the *Gemini*, of Blyth, crew saved; and the *Jamaica*, of London, crew saved.

To the south of Sunderland the storm had claimed more casualties: the *Experiment*, of Stockton, a new ship, was lost near Seaham and all hands perished; the *Maria* was reported on shore near Seaham; the *Francis* was wrecked off the Tees, but the crew saved; a sloop, whose was name was not reported, also came to grief near Seaham with the loss of all her crew; and lastly a Sunderland ship was wrecked, whose name is also unclear, from which at least several men were saved.

Within a week the bodies of the many seamen who had perished in the storm began to be washed up on the North-East coast. They were buried by the different parishes in which they were found.

As well as the frightening power of the sea, sailing ship crews faced other hazards. Excessive drinking of alcohol was a problem with British seamen which continued into the age of steam. Drink ruined the careers and the health of many men. It also contributed to the loss of many ships.

There are numerous accounts of inebriated, sometimes insensible, crews being dumped aboard outward bound sailing ships.

However, while drunkenness caused a lot of trouble amongst crews while ships were in port, or in the early stages of a voyage, the problem usually resolved itself once a vessel was well out to sea and alcohol became unavailable.

The situation with captains was different. Even a teetotal captain would normally have a bottle or two in his cabin for the entertainment of visitors to his ship while in port. But many masters took to drink while at sea.

During June 1857 the South Shields-owned snow *Catherine & Hannah* arrived in the Tyne with the body of her master on board. He had cut his throat with a razor while suffering from what was thought to be delirium tremens through drinking.

Efforts to fight the influence of drink on the lives of sea-

The barque Salween (or Salveen) is driven ashore south of the South Pier at the mouth of the Tyne in November 1895. The Salween was built in Burma of teak and named after a Burmese river. She was sailing for Norwegian owners at the time of her stranding. The ship was being towed into the Tyne by steam tug in rough weather with fierce north-easterly winds blowing when she came to grief. The tow rope broke and she drifted against the end of the South Pier. The vessel was then carried helplessly south of the pier and driven on to the beach. The crew were rescued by breeches buoy and given dry clothing and coffee by the South Shields Volunteer Life Brigade at their headquarters on the pier.

men were made by a number of church and charitable institutions. On the Tyne, the Mission Ship *Joseph Straker*, a former Royal Navy frigate, was established in 1866. One of her chaplains, the Rev S. Streelan, formed a temperance club amongst the pilots and seamen which by 1879 was reported to have 517 members. Six years later the mission opened shore premises at Mill Dam, South Shields.

Another hazard for seamen in the 19th century was disease. Cholera, yellow and other, unspecified, fevers were killers which took the lives of many. Added to these were scurvy, beri-beri, TB and sexually transmitted diseases. Squalid accommodation, insanitary conditions, contaminated food and water, rats and exposure to endemic diseases in the countries which they visited, were all contributory factors.

In September 1854, Captain Luper of the Austrian barque *Germanica*, which had just arrived in the Tyne from London, died of cholera. Several other cases were reported aboard vessels lying in Shields Harbour. Requests were made to the Admiralty and Trinity House for a hulk to be used as a floating hospital, but 17 years were to elapse before this was done.

The year 1866 brought another cholera outbreak. During August, a 22-year-old seaman died of cholera aboard the vessel *Monkwearmouth* as she lay in the Tyne. This collier had just returned from a voyage to the Thames. The man had been ill for 16 hours. Not long afterwards the sloop *Lalla Rookh* came in from Amsterdam with one of her crew dead from the same cause. Two days later the brig *Frederick William* entered the river with the body of another 22-year-old seaman who had fallen victim to cholera.

On 13 October of the same year, the North Shields brig *Elizabeth* was only one day out from the Tyne, on passage towards Altona, when James Willis, a seaman, was found at 8.30pm to be 'fairly sick, vomiting, and purged with cramp in legs and arms'. By 5.30am the following morning he was dead. It was a suspected case of cholera. The unfortunate man was buried at sea.

After being visited by cholera epidemics on four occasions in the 19th century the local authorities on Tyneside took action in 1871 with the creation of the Port of Tyne Sanitary Authority. The crews of all arriving ships were inspected. Any suspected cases were isolated aboard a floating hospital which was moored at Jarrow Slake.

The first of these floating mercy vessels was the *Tyne*, a former ferry, which was fitted out with a 14-bed ward. In time she was joined by a disinfecting hulk and in 1883 a former Dutch vessel named the *Alliance* was converted to take ten patients.

A couple of years later all three hulks were replaced by a purpose-built floating hospital which had been built at Bill Quay, Gateshead. This hospital was also moored at the entrance to Jarrow Slake. Although the sanitary authority had been created to deal specifically with cholera cases, its responsibilities were later expanded to include other conditions such as scurvy, beri-beri and scabies.

Sometimes medical conditions were undiagnosed, but only too real nevertheless to those who suffered them. When launched from Andrew Leslie's Hebburn Shipyard on the Tyne in 1857, the *Nancy Riley* was something of a rare vessel – an iron-built brig. Much of her nine years of life were spent trading to the West Indies and the coast of central America which included several calls at the Mexican port of

Minatitlan for cargoes of mahogany.

In November 1862 the *Nancy Riley* arrived at Plymouth to land a sick seaman at the end of an 84-day passage from Minatitlan. Three of her crew had died. Others were sick. Most had gone down with an unspecified fever on arrival in the West Indies.

Fortunately, a 14-year-old West Indian boy was on board. He had stowed away at Martinique and was free from the 'ague, fever and diarrhoea' which affected the others. With the boy's help, and that of the second mate, the captain managed to navigate the *Nancy Riley* for 30 days as she crossed the Gulf of Mexico and made her way through the Florida Straits.

As more northerly latitudes were reached some of the crew made a partial recovery. However, just before arrival at Plymouth, the ship's carpenter died. Three new seamen were taken aboard to help get the vessel up Channel.

The *Nancy Riley* went on to again visit Mexico and the West Indies. She survived until November 1868 when she was wrecked off St Francis, Guadeloupe.

The wreck of the topsail schooner Luna on the coast near the mouth of the Tyne in June 1897. Unfavourable winds could soon drive a sailing ship ashore. Countless vessels were wrecked in this way, particularly colliers. The Danish-owned Luna had been bound for the Tyne from Finland with timber.

To Foreign Lands

Tyne-owned ships did not always leave from the Tyne and arrive back in the Tyne. They left from many ports worldwide and delivered their cargoes to whatever destinations were required throughout the globe.

Shipbuilder Thomas & William Smith's 'Indiamen' were good examples of the larger Tyne-owned ships which voyaged thousands of miles across oceans. This company had shipbuilding yards at St Peter's in Newcastle and at North Shields.

T&W Smith, as the firm became known, constructed and owned its own fleet of Indiamen. An Indiaman was any vessel which regularly sailed east of the Cape of Good Hope and into the Indian Ocean to trade with India and the Far East. They could vary greatly in size and type of sailing rig. However, Smith's Indiamen were magnificent, full-rigged ships. More often than not they left from the Thames and returned there after the long runs out to the East. But they remained under the ownership of the Tyne-based Smith company.

On 28 February 1831 the firm launched the 608-ton Indiaman *Duke of Northumberland* at its St Peter's yard and over the next 32 years produced a veritable fleet of vessels for the trade to the East. In 1833 the *Duke of Northumberland* was joined by the *Duke of Argyll* and two years later came the *Robert Small* and the *Colombo*.

With the introduction of the 985-ton *Bucephalus* in 1840, T&W Smith now matched the more established London owners for large, magnificent full-rigged ships on the runs to the East.

THOMAS SMITH 1757 – 1836

WILLIAM SMITH 1787 – 1860

Thomas, left, and William Smith, whose shipyard at St Peter's in Newcastle produced many superb full-rigged ships, which they owned and operated as Indiamen trading to the Orient.

The *Bucephalus* was considered a massive vessel for her day and was largely constructed of African oak. The ship had six passenger cabins beneath her poop deck and 15 in the 'tween decks. For more than 20 years she made regular voyages, without serious mishap, between the Thames and India. She had 12 gun ports on each side of the upper deck and 14 on the lower and could easily have been converted into a man-of-war had circumstances warranted it.

Other important Indiamen from Smith's included the 1,031-ton *Ellenborough*, completed in 1842, the 1,051-ton *Gloriana*, of 1843, the 1,562-ton *Marlborough*, of 1845, the 1,667-ton *Blenheim*, of 1848, and the 1,142-ton *Hotspur* of 1851.

The *Hotspur* achieved a particularly good record for regular and swift passage making. In 1855 she sailed from Calcutta to the Thames in 87 days, which included time spent at Cape Town. At the time, this was regarded as one of the fastest runs ever made.

During the 1860s the *Hotspur* was commanded by the distinguished ship master Henry Toynbee. On 23 September, 1863, with him in charge, she arrived off Madras at the end of a smart 83-day passage from Gravesend – 79 from the Lizard.

T&W Smith's ships also did well when pitted

The full-rigged ship Hotspur, one of T&W Smith's Indiamen. She was built at Smith's yard, Newcastle, in 1851. Famed for her fine passage making, the Hotspur was wrecked during a cyclone off Madras (Chenai) in 1872.

On the right, Captain Henry Toynbee, c.1868, commander of the Hotspur and also the Ellenborough and Gloriana.

against similar vessels belonging to competitors in the India trade. In 1849 their *Marlborough*, under the command of Captain J. Webb, left England 12 hours behind the *Alfred*, a large ship belonging to R&H Green of London, but arrived in Calcutta eight days ahead.

These Tyne-built ships attracted much attention. The smart manner in which Smith's *Ellenborough*, commanded by Captain Mark Currie Close, came to anchor off Spithead, Portsmouth, in June 1845 drew complimentary remarks from officers of the Royal Navy. On the following day the Royal Yacht made a point of circling the Indiaman, whose 80-strong crew, immaculately kitted out in white uniforms and straw hats, manned the yards in honour of the occasion.

India was not the only destination visited by Tyne-owned ships – some sailed even further east, to China. Shipowner John Kelso, of North Shields, was the river's most prominent participant in the China tea trade. He chose to go to the shipbuilders of the River Wear at Sunderland for nearly all his clippers. They were constructed at the yard of William Pile.

His first vessel for the China tea trade was the 530-ton full-rigged ship *Kelso*, launched in May 1855. Captain William Coulson took command of this vessel. He was known as a fine passage maker. In the course of her maiden voyage Coulson brought the *Kelso* from Hong Kong to London in 105 days, which put her among the best half dozen passage makers of the 1855-56 tea season. Three years later she clipped three days off this time on a homeward run from Whampoa.

But it is for the extraordinarily fast passage from Anger to Deal that the *Kelso* will always be remembered in sailing ship annals. Anger is situated on the eastern shore of the Banca Strait which separates the islands of Java and Sumatra. It was a landfall and port well known to sailing ships bound both to and from China. The *Kelso* passed there on 30 October 1860 after a mediocre, 41-day, amble from Macao.

But from then on the amble became a headlong gallop. It took just over three weeks to reach the Cape of Good Hope. Six days afterwards St Helena was abeam. On New Year's Day 1861 the *Kelso* came to anchor off Deal – 63 days from Anger. A record, possibly equalled, but never beaten to this day.

Other clippers owned by John Kelso included the *Maitland*, *Undine* and *Deerhound*. A second vessel named the *Kelso* replaced the first from 1861. Their speed performances compared reasonably well with those of the better known China tea clippers such as the *Cutty Sark*, *Taeping* and *Thermopolae*.

However, even though they might be famed for passage making, it was not beneath the dignity of an outward bound clipper to load coal on the North-East coast for some Chinese or intermediate port. On 31 March, 1868, the second *Kelso*, under the command of Captain V. Vowell, left the Tyne with coal for Bombay. On arrival off the Indian port orders were given to discharge at Muscat in Arabia.

From there the *Kelso* went across the Indian Ocean to Penang where general cargo was loaded for Hong Kong, which was reached after beating up the China Sea against the north-east monsoon. After Hong Kong, a call was made at Whampoa where a part cargo of tea was put aboard for London. Loading was completed at Macao and London reached on 17 April, 1869, after a smart 99-day run.

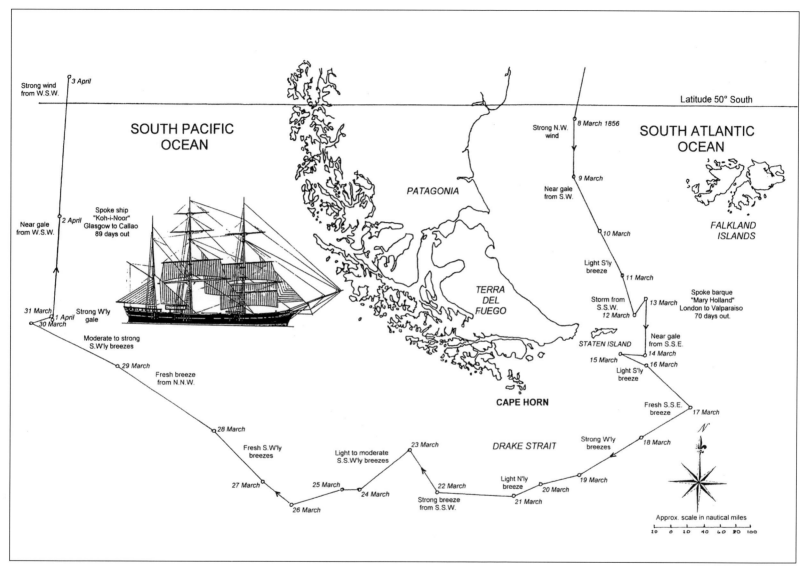

Map drawn by R.E. Keys

The track of the barque Fairy in 1856, from 50° south in the Atlantic, around Cape Horn, to 50° south in the Pacific, when on passage from Malaga, Spain, toward Mazatlan, Mexico (see over page).

During this voyage the second *Kelso* was detained by merchants in harbour for 29 working days and logged 40,064 nautical miles under sail.

Another example of a ship leaving the Tyne with coal and making a long voyage, including rounding Cape Horn, was the barque *Fairy*, which had been built in Hartlepool in 1852.

Commanded by Captain John Gillie, the *Fairy* departed the river with her cargo of 'black diamonds' bound for Genoa, Italy, on 19 July 1855. Her best day's run was 182 miles, achieved when sailing down the coast of Portugal on 10 August. Five days were spent drifting in calms and light winds between Cape Spartel and Cape Trafalgar near the entrance to the Straits of Gibraltar.

While on this section of her voyage the *Fairy* had her rail broken and bulwarks stove in when she was struck by a foreign schooner.

Malaga in southern Spain was passed on 22 August. Genoa was reached on 7 September after a 50-day passage. After Genoa the ship made calls at Marseilles and Barcelona, before going to Malaga where general cargo was loaded for Mazatlan on the Pacific coast of Mexico. Leaving on 19 December she re-entered the Atlantic eight days later and headed towards Cape Horn, the southern tip of South America, notorious for its formidable winds.

The Equator was crossed on 4 February, 1856. It took the ship 26 days to go from 50 degrees south in the Atlantic to 50 degrees south in the Pacific. The vessel rounded Cape Horn in March.

On 19 May, 1856, she anchored off Mazatlan, 153 days out from Malaga. Her best day's run on this passage had been 195 miles, made in the Pacific. The average day's run was just over 86 miles.

After discharging her cargo, the *Fairy* went to Altata in the Gulf of California, Mexico, to load wood and pearl shells for Liverpool.

With Captain Gillie still in command, she sailed on 17 July. Seventy days later her topgallant yard sprung soon

R.F. Gillie

Captain John Gillie, 1829-1906, who commanded the barque Fairy.

after rounding Cape Horn. After an unsuccessful attempt to reach Port William in the Falkland Islands the disabled *Fairy* continued up the Atlantic until on 22 October she dropped anchor at Pernambuco, Brazil. After a two-day stay in the port the ship left on the homeward run for Liverpool. It had been a marathon voyage.

Women at Sea

The departure of an Indiaman, a whaler or any ship setting out on a long voyage would often bring great crowds of spectators and well-wishers to the waterfront to see them off. At such times the Sandhead, on the southern shore of the entrance to the Tyne, would develop an almost carnival-like atmosphere.

It was an occasion when the womenfolk came to fore; the time for mothers, wives and sweethearts to say their fond farewells. Shanties, songs and ditties were sung which invariably alluded to feminine charms.

Tearful young lassies would distribute coloured ribbons amongst the sailors of their fancy. These were used to dress a garland (a hoop of about 12 inches in diameter) which was secured aloft aboard the ship, usually between the fore and main masts, by the youngest of the seamen. It remained in the rigging as a token of farewell until destroyed by the elements.

While all this was going on the captain would be in his cabin entertaining invited friends who had come to accompany him 'over the Bar'. The longer the voyage was expected to be, the greater the number of people invited.

Once the Customs Watch House was passed the seals, which the customs officers had placed on stores of tobacco, wines and spirits, were broken. This was called 'tapping the admiral' and was followed by much eating drinking and merriment.

The guests were usually taken off by tug when a mile or two beyond the Bar. Getting them transferred must have been a lively procedure, especially with those who had imbibed too much. Duckings in the cold waters of the North Sea, or German Ocean as it was commonly referred to in those days, were not unknown.

Ladies among the 'cabin guests' were usually presented with a

An 18th century print: 'The Sailor's Adieu'.

quantity of tea before boarding the tug, while gentlemen freely availed themselves of the duty-free tobacco – a privilege not infrequently abused. It was also the practice to give the tug boat skipper a bottle of rum and a pound of tobacco to share amongst the crew.

Running towards the shore laden with all these 'goodies' demanded a degree of caution. What was being carried was contraband and the Low Lights at North Shields, where the

Customs Watch House was situated, was given a wide berth. Landings were made at the New Quay or at some other wharf lower down the river.

It was a superstitious era. The tug would always move aft when leaving the outward bound ship, great care being taken to avoid crossing her bow. Such a transgression would be construed as inviting ill fortune and portend a calamitous voyage. But once clear, three cheers were given as the last of the canvas was sheeted home aboard the outward bounder as she began her long voyage.

Women, however, were not always left behind when a ship sailed. Many wives who were married to ships' captains shared the joys, hardships and dangers of their husbands' calling. Henry Toynbee, the well-known master who commanded some of T&W Smith's crack Indiamen, often carried his wife with him.

She was the daughter of Rear Admiral William Henry Smyth, a distinguished hydrographer, who Captain Toynbee had come into contact with after writing a paper on lunar observations.

Mrs Toynbee took part in her husband's navigational duties and scientific studies by writing his logs, working sights and drawing some of the microscopic objects which came up in the nets he streamed from his ships from time to time. Some of these were used to illustrate scientific works of the era.

No doubt many wives helped out in similar and other ways, some engaging in more mundane but essential tasks, especially in the smaller vessels where they must have been considered as one of the crew. Sadly, however, the presence of women and their children aboard a ship often only became known as a result of tragedy.

If a ship sank, they would frequently be lost along with the seamen. Examples include:

Barque *Acastus*, September 1869. Foundered when on passage from Queenstown towards London with all hands, including the wife of the master, George Thompson.

Ship *Africa*, January 1879. Wrecked near Tripoli. Wife and 17-year-old daughter of the master, Roger Wood, drowned.

Snow *Albion*, August 1868. Foundered off Beachy Head. Wife and two children of master, John Mervin, drowned.

Schooner *British Settler*, June 1850. Wrecked in Jacobs Bay, South Africa. Wife and three children of master, W.A. Train, drowned or missing.

Snow *Mancio*, May 1835. Wrecked off Blakeney, Norfolk. Wife and four-year-old son of master, Richard Wright, drowned.

Schooner *Lady Saltoun*, September 1851. Disappeared when on passage Tyne to Hamburg. Wife of master, William Jackson, on board.

Among the stories of women who went to sea, that of Mary Ann Arnold, the daughter of a Royal Navy lieutenant, is one of the more colourful. At the age of 10, while living in Sheerness at the mouth of the Thames, a boy she knew lent her an old jacket, trousers and shirt. Dressing in these, she presented herself to the master of the Sunderland collier *Williams*, which was lying in Sheerness, and asked for a job. He took her on as a cabin boy. For more than two years she served on the *Williams* in which time six different captains came and went.

The seventh master she did not get on well with which

caused her to look for another berth. In August 1838 she shipped aboard the snow *Anne* at Shields for a voyage to London and Quebec. The *Anne* belonged to Thomas and George Metcalfe of South Shields. Mary remained with her until June 1839 when, during a gale, she stranded on the Sherringham Shoal, off Norfolk, while on passage from the Tyne towards London. All on board got ashore safely.

Returning to Shields, Mary next found a berth as a cabin boy aboard the snow *Choice*, which belonged to T&W Smith. The *Choice* was given the job of carrying stores from the Tyne to Smith's full-rigged ship, the *Robert Small*, lying in the London River and preparing for a voyage to the

East. By this time Mary Anne had been at sea for about three years. It was time for promotion. The *Robert Small* required a seaman. Mary was in the right place at the right time. It was an easy matter to transfer between vessels belonging to the same company.

The *Robert Small* set out on her Indian voyage carrying general cargo, passengers and Mary. Her master was later to recall that during a heavy gale in the Bay of Biscay he had seen 'Miss Arnold amongst the first to go aloft to reef the mizzen topgallant sail'. By this time Mary Anne was 15 years old. While on the voyage, in September 1839, it was discovered that the enthusiastic seaman was a girl! Mary Anne's days as an ordinary sailor were over.

Praised by passengers and crew, she was given a cabin and

the lady passengers showered her with clothing and presents. The *Robert Small*'s captain promised to pay her wages for the round trip. The bashful Mary became the centre of attention. Always sure of an audience, she was frequently called upon to 'spin a yard' about her life as a cabin boy and seaman. Just what went through the minds of her former fellow sailors, as she promenaded the quarter deck with the lady passengers, is not recorded.

Mary had two brothers serving in the Royal Navy as petty officers. One of them was aware that his sister had gone to sea but had kept her secret. It would be fascinating to know what became of the resourceful Mary – one can only hope that life went well for her.

Left, a fishing boat, probably a Scottish 'fifey' sails down the Tyne around 1898. At the far right is the training ship Wellesley. In the distance are the masts of many more sailing vessels.

Right, a three-masted barque is towed towards harbour by a tug around the same year. She is probably Scandinavian.

These photographs are both from lantern slides.

Tragedy and Ordeal

Many passengers as well as seamen were lost in shipping tragedies. Among the most harrowing stories is that of the Tyne-built barque *Exmouth*, which belonged to John Eden and Joseph Nixon of South Shields. In her 30 years of life she had served as a Greenland whaler and general trader before returning to carrying North Atlantic emigrants.

On 25 April 1847, under the command of Captain Isaac Booth, with a crew of ten, the *Exmouth* sailed from Londonderry in the north of Ireland. She was bound for Quebec in Canada. A little under 97ft long and 28ft wide, in her hold were crammed 240 impoverished Irish men, women and children desperate to escape the famine which had engulfed their homeland.

Many of the women and children were on their way to be reunited with husbands and fathers who were already in the New World. There were also three cabin passengers – young, unmarried, middle class women.

At 4pm, when land was just out of sight, the wind suddenly veered to the north and brought with it a howling gale. Several sails were blown from their bolt ropes. During the forenoon watch on Monday a heavy sea crashed on board, lifting the long boat from its chocks, washing away the lifeboat and smashing the bulwarks.

On Tuesday the gale was still howling with no sign of a let-up. At 11pm a light was sighted. Captain Booth thought it was Tory Island off the north coast of Ireland. He was mistaken. It turned out to be the light marking Cape Orsay on the southern tip of the Rinns of Islay in the Inner Hebrides.

Drawn by R.E. Keys

The emigrant ship Exmouth is wrecked on rocks on the coast of Islay in the Inner Hebrides after leaving Londonderry. Over 100 lives were lost.

The storm had driven the *Exmouth* a long way to the north and west. Soon broken water, denoting shallows or rocks, was sighted all around.

At 12.30am on Wednesday the ship struck rocks. The main mast then collapsed towards the shore, providing a bridge to the rocky crags near the wreck. Three South Shields men, John Stevens, William Coulthard and George Lighthouse scrambled ashore. Captain Booth tried to follow but was washed away by a large wave – another was soon to sever the main mast escape route.

The Shields men were to witness the terrible end of the *Exmouth*. She was dragged down into the sea. Most of the passengers were still below. They were all lost. On Thursday the sea began to give up its dead. Twenty bodies drifted ashore – the majority women or girls still in their night-clothes. In time, 108 bodies were recovered.

The *Exmouth* was only certified to carry 165 emigrants. A loophole in the law allowed children to count as half an adult, or less, which accounted for the extra 75 thought to have been on board.

In reporting the tragedy, the *Illustrated London News* commented in gentle tone: 'They were all buried in a beautiful spot – soft green turf, surrounded by wild rocks.'

Another episode among many which showed how bad conditions could be for Irish emigrants was the voyage of the 330-ton barque *Elizabeth & Sarah*, commanded by and belonging to Andrew Simpson, of North Shields. In July 1846 she put to sea from the tiny port of Killala, Co Mayo, with 276 desperate souls aboard anxious to reach North America and escape the ravages of the Irish potato famine. There were 64 more people aboard than appeared on the passenger list

The Illustrated London News reported on the tragedy of the Exmouth. This picture shows the rocks which the ill-fated ship struck, and the recovery of the bodies.

which had been certified by an immigration officer.

Only 32 berths were available. Communal sleeping in extremely overcrowded conditions must have been the only alternative to sleeping on the open deck. There were no sanitary arrangements of any description.

Once underway, other serious shortcomings soon became apparent. Fresh water was in short supply. Only 70 per cent of what should have been carried, according to the 1842 Passenger Act, was on board, and that was stowed in leaky casks.

Each emigrant should have been issued with 7lbs of provisions per week, but none was ever forthcoming. All too soon conditions below deck became insanitary.

The *Elizabeth & Sarah* had put to sea in a deplorable state. For five long weeks she wrestled with the vagaries of the North Atlantic. Partially dismasted, hardly manageable, with her emigrants wracked by fever, starving, suffering from thirst and 42 of them dead, the ship somehow reached the entrance to the St Lawrence River.

Her plight became known to the Canadian authorities but relief was slow in coming. There was much dithering. Government regulations did not provide for a tug to be sent to her aid.

The only person to show compassion towards the unfortunate passengers aboard the *Elizabeth & Sarah* was a man called Alexander Carlisle Buchanan. Learning of their plight, he cut through the red tape and sent a steamer, at his own expense, to bring her in.

The saga of the ancient *Elizabeth & Sarah* did not end when her emaciated emigrants were carried or staggered ashore. A cargo of timber was loaded at Quebec for the Tyne where she arrived on 27 October 1846 at the end of a heavy weather passage with her stern stove in, bulwarks washed away and a damaged rudder.

She went on to roam the seas for another 12 years before being abandoned in the North Atlantic. The ship was 96 years old at the time of her loss.

An advertisement for emigrants to South Australia in The Newcastle Daily Journal, *March 1846.*

The Conrad Connection

The Tyne and its ships form an inextricable part in the sea life of Joseph Conrad, the distinguished novelist, ship master and teller of maritime tales.

He first saw its shores through the eyes of an ordinary seaman while serving aboard the Lowestoft schooner *Skimmer of the Sea* when she entered the river in the summer of 1878 to collect a cargo of coal to deliver to her home port. Conrad was to make two more visits to the river aboard the *Skimmer of the Sea*. He was later to recount his impressions of what can only be the Tyne in his novel, *Mirror of the Sea*, published in 1906.

With his classic story *Youth* (1902), Conrad has left us an incomparable narrative of a voyage to the East aboard a wooden sailing ship carrying a cargo of coal.

The grimy *Judea*, described in the novel, and which Conrad came to love, was in reality the barque *Palestine*, built in 1857 by Pickersgill & Miller of Sunderland for Robert Morrison of South Shields.

With Conrad serving on board as second mate, the *Palestine*, under the command of Captain E. Beard, left Gravesend bound for the Tyne in September 1881 and ran slap into a series of gales which kept her 'knocking about' in the North Sea for 22 days before the sanctuary of Shields Harbour was reached on 20 October. It was a portent of things to come.

It was not until late November that the ship set sail

The great novelist Joseph Conrad, who visited the Tyne in sailing ships on several occasions and mentioned the river in his writings.

again. She departed the Tyne bound for Bangkok with 557 tons of West Hartley coal in her hold.

All went well until the *Palestine* cleared the Channel and was nosing her way into the Atlantic. Then another run of gale force winds tore away much of her canvas. On Christmas Eve a leak was discovered. Sixteen days later the much mangled ship limped into Falmouth for repairs. Eight months were spent in the Cornish port, where the cargo of coal had to be discharged and reloaded before the voyage could be resumed.

The passage to the east was a slow one. On 11 March 1882, after 173 days at sea, when off Bangka Island in the Java Sea, a strong smell resembling paraffin was noticed. During the following day smoke was discovered coming from the coal on the port side of the main hatch. Water was poured into the hold. Later an attempt was made to heave the heated coal overboard. Only about four tons had been got rid of when a coal gas explosion damaged the lower deck.

The boats were provisioned and the *Palestine* headed for the coast of Sumatra. At 3pm on the afternoon of 14 March the steamer *Somerset* came alongside. Later, a tow rope was got aboard but, wafted by the stream of air caused by the forward motion, the fire began to increase rapidly. The *Somerset* was asked to tow the *Palestine* ashore, but the request was refused.

At 11pm the *Palestine* was abandoned. Her crew got clear in three boats. Conrad took charge of the smallest with a crew of three men. The flotilla made for Muntok, on Bangka Island, which was reached safely at 10pm on the night of 15 March. After six days ashore they were picked up by the

The Tyne at North Shields, late 19th century.

British steamer *Sissie* which took them to Singapore.

A Court of Enquiry, convened at Singapore on 2 April, held that the cause of the fire was spontaneous combustion and that the vessel was not abandoned prematurely. No blame was attached to the officers or crew.

It was the humble barque *Palestine* which introduced Joseph Conrad to the Malay Archipelago, the setting for some of his best writing. It also showed him the workings of a Court of Enquiry, which set the scene for his famed novel *Lord Jim*. Without the *Palestine* the world of literature would have been much the poorer.

Five-masters in the Tyne

From about the middle of the 19th century, up until the outbreak of the First World War, many thousands of tons of coal and coke were exported from the Tyne, around Cape Horn, to the west coast of South America in the holds of sailing ships. But, rather surprisingly given their prime position at the departure point, very few Tyne owners became involved.

John Brunton of Tynemouth was an exception. His only ship, the iron-hulled barque *Adelaide*, built on the Tyne in 1875, made a number of voyages to South America, some of them from the river of her birth. On 4 May 1884 the *Adelaide* left Tyne Dock under the command of Captain William Raeburn, bound for Valparaiso in Chile, with a crew of 18 and 1,110 tons of Tanfield Moor coal. A steamer 'spoke' to her in the latitude of the Canary Islands on 28 May, but afterwards neither she nor her crew were ever seen again.

The Cape Horn trade, so neglected by Tyne shipowners, was taken up by others from outside the region and abroad. By the 1880s the surviving Tyne-owned sailing ships found themselves dwarfed in their native river by great iron and steel built full-rigged ships and barques with cargo capacities to match their size.

They represented deepwater sail's last attempt to thwart the advance of steam. The most distinctive of them all were

R.E. Keys Collection

Impressive five-master. The French steel five-masted barque France (1) alongside coal staiths at the Albert Edward Dock, North Shields.

those belonging to the French shipowning firm of Anton Bordes. The company's ships were real beauties.

Bordes' large, yet graceful *France* was the first merchantman ever to be rigged as a five-masted barque. Only six merchant five-masted barques were ever built and four visited the Tyne. The *France* was able to carry well over 5,000 tons of coal, an enormous amount in those days. Under all plain sail she spread 49,000 square feet of canvas.

When this magnificent vessel entered the Tyne for the first time on a fine March day in 1892 many sightseers gathered to see her come in. Captain E. Voisin, her justifiably proud master, opened his ship to the public at threepence per head, with the proceeds going to the Tynemouth Jubilee Infirmary.

Then, with a cargo of coal loaded at the Albert Edward Dock, North Shields, she ran out to Valparaiso, Chile, in the splendid time of 76 days. Such fine passages were the norm for the majestic *France*.

The ship again visited the Tyne to load coal in 1895, 1899 and 1901. On 14 March, 1901, the *France* departed the river for Valparaiso, again with a cargo of coal. On 10 May she encountered a fierce storm off the South American coast and began listing heavily. Her cargo shifted and soon she was taking in water. The next day the crew abandoned ship. They

Courtesy of Tyne & Wear Museums

In this picture the France (1) shows her graceful lines to good effect as she lies in the Albert Edward Dock to load coal.

were all rescued by a German barque and landed safely at Valparaiso.

The *France* was last seen by a Spanish vessel drifting half-capsized several hundred miles off the River Plate. She was never sighted again.

However, a second five-masted barque named the *France* was completed for a Rouen firm in 1911. At the time of her completion she was described as the largest sailing ship ever built.

The second *France* arrived in the Tyne on 10 September, 1919, for repairs to be carried out. After these were completed she left the river to cross the Atlantic to Baltimore, USA, with a cargo of coal. She was towed by a tug down the North Sea coast, but the tow rope parted during a strong gale. The ship managed to survive this incident and put into Leith in Scotland. In early February 1920 she again sailed for Baltimore.

The second *France* was lost two years later on a coral reef in the Pacific while bound for New Caledonia.

The five-masted barque France (2) leaving the Tyne on 1 December 1919 under the tow of the tug Joffre.

The five-masted barque *R.C. Rickmers* was a German-owned vessel with auxiliary steam engines. She visited the Tyne on two occasions, in 1909 and 1910. On each occasion she loaded over 6,000 tons of coke for San Francisco.

On the outbreak of the Second World War in 1914 the *R.C. Rickmers* was in Cardiff where she had arrived to load a cargo of coal. She was promptly seized by the authorities.

The ship was later bought by Welsh owners and renamed *Neath*.

The fourth five-masted barque to visit the Tyne was the ill-fated Danish vessel *Kobenhavn*. Like the other giant barques of this type she had a steel hull. She was also equipped with an auxiliary diesel engine from Burmeister & Wain and had a spread of sails which totalled 56,000 sq feet.

The *Kobenhavn* was launched in March 1921 at Leith,

Scotland, for the Danish East Asiatic Line, of Copenhagen. She was to be the company's training ship for officers and was also intended to carry cargo so that she could earn an income.

After completion at Leith in the early autumn of 1921 the vessel sailed across the North Sea to Copenhagen where she was visited by over 12,000 people, including the King and Queen of Denmark. Afterwards, she re-crossed the North Sea and arrived in the Tyne on 31 October 1921. Berthing at Tyne Dock, during her stay in the river the *Kobenhavn* was visited by Prince Axel, nephew of the Danish king, himself a shipmaster and in command of the Danish East Asiatic line's motorship *Fiona*.

The *Kobenhavn* left the Tyne on 17 November 1921 with a cargo of 3,000 tons of coke and 750 tons of fire-proof stones destined for Honolulu. Her first port of call was Antwerp.

The ship put in sterling service for another seven years, but was eventually lost in tragic circumstances. In December 1928 she departed Buenos Aires on passage for Melbourne in ballast. There were 60 crew on board, comprising 45 cadets, officers, seamen, a doctor and catering personnel. The *Kobenhavn* and her crew were never seen again.

Another interesting but ill-fated visitor to the Tyne was the barque *Killoran*. She was launched at Troon, Scotland, in 1900, and came to the river on 24 July 1938 with a cargo of grain from Australia. This was probably the last time that a deep-water square-rigged ship ever entered the Tyne laden with a commercial cargo. At this time she was Finnish-owned.

The Danish five-masted barque Kobenhavn in the Tyne in November 1921, probably at Tyne Dock.

After discharging, the *Killoran* left on 13 August bound for Mahe in the Seychelle Islands of the Indian Ocean to load guano for Auckland, New Zealand. It took her 156 days to reach Mahe from the Tyne and a further 74 days to get to Auckland.

Tragically, the *Killoran* was lost during the Second World War when she was sunk by the German commerce raider *Widder*, a converted merchant ship, on 10 August 1940. She went down with all sails set, which must have been a sad sight. However, no lives were lost. The crew were taken aboard the German vessel.

The Finnish barque Killoran loosens sails as she is towed out of the Tyne in August 1938 bound for the Seychelle Islands. She was probably the last square-rigged sailing ship to bring a commercial cargo to the Tyne.

Training Ship Visitors

The Tyne has witnessed visits by many sail training ships over a long period. Indeed, the river once had its own training vessels, but these were stationery and did not put to sea. They were both named HMS *Wellesley* and were former Royal Navy ships used to educate and train boys who were 'homeless, destitute or neglected'. Many were probably orphans.

The first *Wellesley* (originally named *Cornwall*) had been built as a 74-gun warship, being launched at Deptford, London, in 1812. In 1868 she was given to Tyneside local authorities for use as a training ship under the terms of the Reformatory and Industrial Schools Act of 1866. She arrived in the Tyne in June 1868 under tow of the steam tug *Scotia*. The *Wellesley* was moored at North Shields, directly opposite the New Quay.

Commander Pocock, RN, was appointed superintendent of the floating school. At a meeting held on board, it was resolved to start with 25 boys, although eventually up to 200 could be accommodated. The meeting also decided to advertise for a schoolmaster who was to be 'required to live on board and amongst his other qualifications he must have a knowledge of music and be able to play the harmonium'.

When the large full-rigged ship *Bosphorus* sailed from the Tyne in October 1869, bound for Alexandria, she had on board the first boy from the *Wellesley* 'apprenticed at sea'. As she passed the training ship 'her boys gave a hearty cheer for their late comrade which was responded to by the *Bosphorus*'.

The boys of the second training ship Wellesley man the yards at her North Shields mooring c.1880.

The second Wellesley at North Shields c.1900. The High Light can be seen behind the ship and the Low Light on the right of the picture. Many of the boys trained aboard her went on to have seafaring careers. The vessel on the right is the RNR training ship Castor.

When the barque *Britannia* caught fire while lying in Northumberland Dock boys from the *Wellesley* helped to fight the blaze.

Serving aboard the training vessel was not to the liking of every lad. In June 1871 the *Newcastle Daily Journal* reported that 14-year-old Joseph Lupton had absconded from a picnic party at Whitley Bay and a one pound reward was offered for information leading to his return.

A replacement for the first *Wellesley* arrived in the Tyne in October 1873. The old ship was returned to the Admiralty and scrapped.

The second *Wellesley* had originally been named the *Boscawen*, being launched at Woolwich Dockyard in 1844. She had been an extraordinary 18 years on the stocks before the launch.

Boys take part in cutlass drill on the deck of the second Wellesley *c.1900*

In 1883 she was shifted from a berth off the Limekiln Shore, North Shields, not far from the entrance to the Albert Edward Dock, to No 3 Tier, about 50 yards above the Royal Naval Reserve training ship *Castor*.

In 1891 the second *Wellesley's* captain superintendent, Commander Hugh Ryder, wrote to the *Newcastle Daily Journal* about a problem he was experiencing: 'The ship is within ear shot of Low Street … the language heard from the shore (particularly on Saturday nights) is very often blasphe-

mous and filthy. This language is sometimes addressed to the ship and frequently the port sashes have to be kept closed on the side of the ship nearest the shore to prevent boys listening to it.

'This sort of thing also occurs on a Sunday in the evening when the boys are at Divine Service, in summer, when boat loads of noisy, ill-behaved girls amuse themselves by serenading the ship and calling out to any boys they may see.'

The commander added: 'Every year there have been cases

in the summer of boys clandestinely visiting the shore to mix up in the street play of the young girls going about the fish quay. The boys then absent were caught swimming off to the ship after dark.'

The boys normally spent four years on the *Wellesley*. Many went on to have seafaring careers. In 1911, for example, 44 left to join British and foreign merchant vessels and 14 were recruited into the Royal Navy.

This second training vessel's career was to end abruptly on 11-12 March, 1914, when fire broke out in the ship's drying room. It soon gained hold and the *Wellesley* was gutted despite action from fireboats and other craft. She sank in 30 feet of water. Her trainees and instructors were safely rescued by lifeboat and the tug *Vigilant*. Eventually, the ship was refloated and towed to Blyth for breaking up.

The end of the Wellesley. Fire engulfs the ship in March 1914. The vessel was gutted by the blaze and later towed to Blyth where she was broken up.

One of the earliest seagoing sail training ships recorded as visiting the Tyne was the *Mathilda,* a Belgian barque. She entered the river on 9 September 1867 to replenish water casks. At the time it was reported that she was a training vessel for Belgian boys and was cruising the North Sea. She had come from Iceland.

Other early visits by sail training ships to the Tyne included the *Grand Duchess Maria Nikolaevna,* a Russian three-masted full-rigged ship with an iron hull. Completed at Greenock on the Clyde in 1873, she was bought by the Odessa School of Navigation in 1899 for use as a sail training ship and re-named the *Grand Duchess Maria Nikolaevna,* after the third daughter of Tsar Nicholas II.

She first came to the Tyne in 1913 for an extensive refit at the Wallsend shipyard of Swan Hunter & Wigham Richardson. After the Russian Revolution of 1917 the ship managed to stay out of Bolshevik hands and continued sailing under Russian Republic colours.

A view of the Russian sail training ship Grand Duchess Maria Nikolaevna looking forward from the poop deck

The *Grand Duchess Maria Nikolaevna* returned to the Tyne in 1920 to have her cadet-ship furnishings stripped out so that she could be used as a cargo vessel. Afterwards, she departed the river for Montreal where timber was loaded for Liverpool. In 1921 she was acquired by a London company and renamed *Silvana*. However, the following year she was sold to Italian shipbreakers.

The first sail training vessel to visit the river after the Second World War was the lovely little Norwegian full-rigged ship *Sorlandet*. She arrived in the Tyne during July 1948. Her attractive appearance, plus the smart turnout and good conduct of her merchant navy cadets, endeared her to the hearts of many Tynesiders.

The *Sorlandet*'s week-long stay certainly enlivened the Newcastle Quayside scene of the day. It was the ship's first post-war visit to Britain. The vessel was built at Kristiansand, southern Norway, being completed in 1927.

During the Second World War the *Sorlandet* had fallen into German hands. While at Kirkenes in northern Norway in c.1942 she was damaged by a Russian bomb and slowly sank, with only her masts protruding above the water.

But the Germans raised her and she became, minus her masts, an accommodation vessel at Kristiansand. After the war, she was returned to Norwegian owners and completely refitted to restart her career as a sail training ship. The *Sorlandet* was not fitted with engines until the mid-1950s. The authors believe she is still afloat and serving as a school ship at Kristiansand.

Another fascinating training vessel to arrive in the river was the Brazilian Navy's four-masted barquentine *Almirante Saldanha*. This ship had been launched by Vickers

The Grand Duchess Maria Nikolaevna pictured leaving the Tyne in 1913.

Armstrongs at Barrow in December 1933. She visited the Tyne in September 1950 and came in from Norway. On her way across the North Sea the *Almirante Saldanha* lost her bowsprit in a gale. Furthermore, her stay in the river was delayed by engine trouble.

The ship left the river on 27 September bound for Amsterdam. She had originally come to Europe for a refit by her builders and the opportunity was taken for her to visit a number of ports before returning to Brazil. Her rigging was removed in 1964 when she became a full-powered oceanographic research vessel.

September 1957 saw the Danish training vessel *Danmark* berth in the Tyne. This full-rigged ship is still sailing and is equipped with an auxiliary engine. Built in 1933, the *Danmark* is considered by many of the old sailing ship men as the most attractively designed of the 'modern' sail training vessels, incorporating, as she does, many traditional features.

At least one sail training ship was built on the Tyne. She was the *General Baquedano*, constructed by Armstrong Whitworth at their Elswick Yard, Newcastle.

The *General Baquedano* was designed by Sir Philip Watts for the Chilean Navy as a training vessel for seamanship, naval engineering and gunnery. She performed this role for 60 years, 40 of which were as an active, ocean-going ship, showing her country's flag in many parts of the world. As a warship, the vessel was not without teeth. Her armament consisted of four 4.7-inch guns, two Maxim machine guns and two 12-

Crowds flock to see the Norwegian training ship Sorlandet at Newcastle Quayside in July 1948.

The Chilean navy training ship General Baquedano off the Tyne in 1899. The vessel was built on the Tyne at Armstrong Whitworth's Elswick shipyard, Newcastle.

pounder and two 6-pounder guns. The vessel was equipped with triple expansion engines from Hawthorn Leslie's St Peter's Works, Newcastle.

Launched at 4.30pm on the rainy afternoon of 5 July 1898, the ship was named by Madame Bascunan, wife of the Secretary of the Chilean Legation in London. Her commander designate, Captain Lorrain, watched her slide into the river without mishap. After calling at the French naval base of Brest, the *General Baquedano* left Europe for Chile during November 1899.

One unusual incident connected with the vessel occurred in Sydney, Australia, in 1903. In a street fracas, one of her seamen allegedly bit off a man's finger. Arrested for the alleged offence, he was later released after a bond of £60 had been entered into.

This affair coincided with the introduction of a new and controversial Aliens Act in Australia which in effect prevented the seaman from remaining ashore to face trial but if he left the £60 would be forfeited.

In due course the trial date came, but the seaman was aboard the *General Baquedano,* then in New Zealand waters. The bond was forfeited, but the judge, recognising the absurdity of the situation, ordered the money to be refunded. The Chilean authorities did offer to send the accused man back – an offer which was declined by the Australian attorney general.

The *General Baquedano* made her final overseas voyage in 1935. During the following year she was given permanent moorings off the Chilean naval base at Talcahuano where she was used as an instruction centre for trainee seamen. It must have been at about this time that her yards were removed

F.A.C. Keys

The training ship Danmark dries her sails at Newcastle Quayside in September 1957.

from her main mast. By the 1950s the condition of her hull had deteriorated to such an extent that it was obvious the old ship could not remain afloat much longer. She was broken up in c.1958.

Arguably, the *General Baquedano* was the last square-rigged sailing ship to built on the Tyne. Many would claim that the powerful steam engines with which she was fitted debar her from that distinction, the real claimant being the *Lydgate*, a large, engine-less, four-masted barque, launched from Palmers' Howdon Yard on 28 September 1893.

Last of the Long-haul Traders

The distinction of being the last long-haul, engineless sailing ship to be owned and registered on the Tyne must go to the *Ravenscraig*. In September 1896 this iron, full-rigged ship became the property of Thomas Mabane, a South Shields solicitor. She had been built on the Clyde about 30 years earlier.

In the course of her first voyage as a Tyne ship the *Ravenscraig*, under Captain Purvis, caused great anxiety by taking 185 days to sail from Port Townsend, in the state of Washington, along the west coast of North and South America to Callao in Peru. The usual passage time for this 4,800-mile run was 70 days.

Following Mabane's death in 1899 ownership of the *Ravenscraig* was vested in a 'one ship' company, bearing her own name, with John Moralee Junior as manager. He eventually became owner just before her sale to Norwegian interests in April 1901. This transaction brought to an end the Tyne's participation in the long-haul sailing ship trades. Never more would the harbours of the Americas, East Indies, China, Japan or the Antipodes play host to the lofty, wind-driven ships bearing the words Newcastle, North Shields or South Shields on their sterns.

Courtesy of South Tyneside MBC

A vessel very similar to the Ravenscraig, the Finnish barque Winterhude leaves the Tyne in 1934. She had just discharged a cargo of grain from Australia. She was returning to her home port in the Alund Islands, Finland, and is riding high out of the water without any cargo on board, just ballast for stability.

The Tall Ships Races

Graphic Photo Union

The idea of organising an international sail training race was first suggested around 1953. The course the ships were to follow was from the Bahamas to the Bristol Channel. Although this ambitious scheme was never realised, the seeds had been planted, and within a couple of years the Sail Training Ship International Race Committee had been set up.

On 7 July 1956 the first Tall Ships Race set off with a course from Torbay to Lisbon and the description 'tall ship' was coined. Some 20 ships from 11 nations took part, including the Norwegian full-rigged ships *Sorlandet* and *Christian Radich*, and the Danish-owned *Georg Stage*, which have all visited the Tyne in recent years. Most interesting to Tynesiders, that first race included the Swedish-owned *Flying Clipper*, formerly the yacht *Sunbeam*, once the property of Tyne shipowner Walter Runciman.

Since the 1956 event Tall Ships Races have taken place every year in many parts of the world and the Tyne has been graced by these lovely vessels on several occasions.

Flying Clipper, previously Sunbeam. The elegant three-masted schooner yacht was completed, with luxurious specifications, in 1929. In 1942 she was taken over by the Royal Navy and in 1946 sold to Sweden as a training ship. In 1955 she was sold to the Clipper Line and renamed Flying Clipper.

Derek Henderson

The Russian four-masted barque Krusenstern in the Tyne in 1993. She was completed in 1926 at Wesermunde as the Padua for Ferdinand Laeisz owner of the famous Flying 'P' Line of Hamburg as a fine cargo ship. Accommodation was provided for 40 cadets who received a very practical training on this pure square-rigged sailing ship, the last of her type to be built for a western owner. Laeisz never fitted engines to any of his sailing ships, which managed very well without them. Padua clocked up some very fast speeds, notably only 65 days from the English Channel to the Spencer Gulf, Australia, in 1933. After World War II Padua was seized by the USSR and renamed Krusenstern. After 20 years as a pure sailing ship Krusenstern was fitted with a motor engine and became a very effective non-cargo carrying training ship.

Inset: Krusenstern in her pre-war prime as Padua (Real Photographs Co. Ltd.).

R.E. Keys

The Statsraad Lehmkuhl in the Tyne in 1993. This steel barque was completed in 1914 as the Grossherzog Friedrich August, for the German Schoolship Association. With space for 240 cadets and a 600 horse-power auxiliary engine, she never relied on sail alone. After World War I she was ceded to Britain as war reparation and acquired by the Newcastle firm J. Coull & Sons to be converted to a cargo vessel. A collapse in freight rates scuppered this plan and she never sailed as a Tyne-owned ship. She was acquired by Norwegian owners in 1923 as a training ship and renamed Statsraad Lehmkuhl. During World War II Germany used her as a depot ship and renamed her Westwärs. After the war she returned to Norway and now undertakes occasional voyages for the Bergen Schoolship Association, visiting the Tyne in 1987 and 1993.

The four-masted barque Sedov off the Tyne in 1993. She was built in 1921 at Kiel as the Magdalen Vinnen, a cargo ship. She was sold and renamed Kommodore Johnsen in 1936. Because she was fitted with a motor engine, pre-war sailing ship enthusiasts were not as fond of her as of ships which relied on wind power alone. In 1945 the Kommodore Johnsen was allocated to the USSR as war reparation and renamed Sedov, and she was converted into a training ship.

Sailing Ship Rigs and Rigging

The classification of sailing ship rigs and rigging is a contentious one which has exercised a lot of minds in recent years. There were many variations on a theme, particularly in respect of the smaller vessels the description of whose rigs were sometimes determined by the perceptions of their builders, owners or masters. What was one man's sloop could be another man's smack or cutter. It was not uncommon for brigantines to be referred to as brigs; snows were almost universally described as brigs, except in shipping registers and advertisements. On occasions barquentines were referred to simply as brigantines or, more specifically, three-masted brigantines. The description 'barquentine' was also applied to some three-mast topsail schooners which carried a standing square sail on the fore yard. It was all very much of a potpourri; our maritime forefathers did not seem unduly concerned about the minutiae of rig classification.

However, from about the second quarter of the 19th century, British registered merchant ships were classified according to rig. This was entered on their Custom House Registers, in the listings of Lloyd's Register of Shipping and other directories of that genre. About ten specific types of rig were represented among the Tyne sailing ships. There were something like 400 full-rigged ships (usually referred to as simply 'ship' rigged), 1,285 barques, 875 brigs, 1,450 snows, three hermaphrodites, nine barquentines, 145 brigantines, 455 schooners, 95 sloops, and ten ketches. Also listed were three vessels described as 'keel' and three as 'smack' rigged.

The following is an explanation of rigs as understood by the authors. They may vary in some minor details from definitions used in 'tall ship' and yachting circles of the present day.

R.E. Keys

The full-rigged Danish Training ship Georg Stage passes North Shields under sail during the Tall Ships visit to the Tyne in 1986.

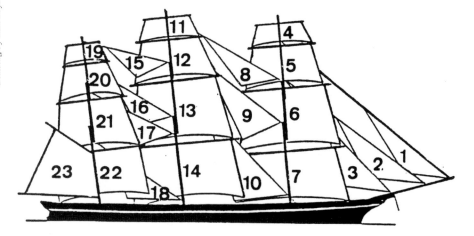

Ship: *a full-rigged ship has three or more masts. Square-rigged on all masts. The Tyne ship-rigged vessels never exceeded three masts.*

1. Flying-jib
2. Jib
3. Fore-topmast-staysail
4. Fore-royal
5. Fore-top-gallant-sail
6. Fore-topsail

7. Fore-sail or fore-course
8. Main-royal-staysail
9. Main-topgallant-staysail
10. Main-top-mast-staysail
11. Main-royal
12. Main-topgallant-sail

13. Main-topsail
14. Main-sail or main-course
15. Mizzen-royal-staysail
16. Mizzen-topgallant-staysail
17. Mizzen-topgallant staysail
18. Mizzen-staysail

19. Mizzen-royal
20. Mizzen-topgallant-sail
21. Mizzen-topsail
22. Crossjack
23. Spanker

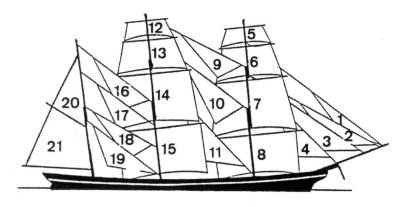

Barque: *a barque has three or more masts. Square-rigged on all masts except the aftermost which is for-and-aft rigged. All the Tyne owned barques were three-masted.*

1. Flying-jib
2. Outer-jib
3. Inner-jib
4. Fore-topmast-stay-sail
5. Fore-royal
6. Fore-topgallant-sail
7. Fore-top-sail
8. Fore-sail or fore-course
9. Main-royal-stay-sail
10. Main-topgallant-stay-sail
11. Main-topmast-staysail

12. Main-royal
13. Main-topgallant sail
14. Main-topsail
15. Main-sail or main-course
16. Mizzen-topgallant staysail
17. Mizzen-topmast staysail
18. Mizzen-middle staysail
19. Mizzen-staysail
20. Gaff-topsail
21. Spanker

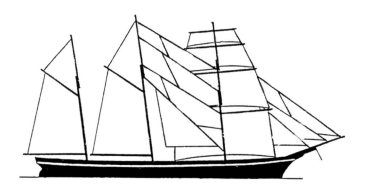

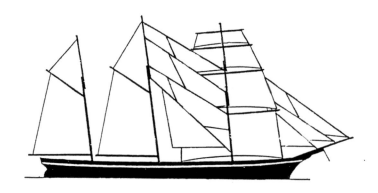

Barquentine: *a barquentine, occasionally referred to as a brigantine, has three or more masts. Square-rigged on the fore-mast, fore-and-aft rigged on the remainder. Only two Tyne-owned barquentines were four-masted.*

Brigantine: *a brigantine has two masts. Square-rigged on the fore-mast; fore-and-aft on the main-mast.*

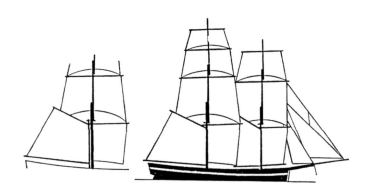

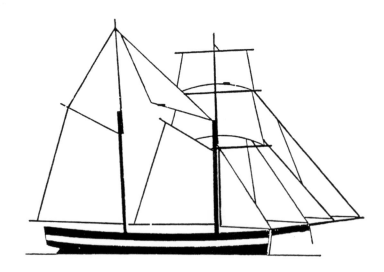

Snow and brig: *a snow (left) and a brig. A brig has two masts, both square-rigged. A snow was identical to a brig except that a trysail mast was fitted immediately behind the lower main-mast from which the spanker was set.*

Topsail-schooner: *a schooner or topsail-schooner has two or more masts. Fore-and-aft rigged with square topsails on the fore-mast.*

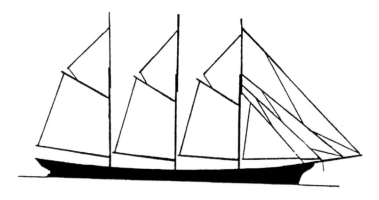

Fore-and-aft schooner: *a fore-and-aft schooner has two or more masts. All fore-and-aft rigged.*

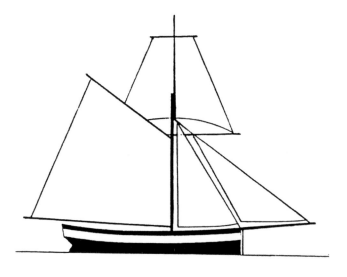

Sloop: *a sloop has just one mast. Fore-and-aft rigged. Some would have carried a square topsail.*

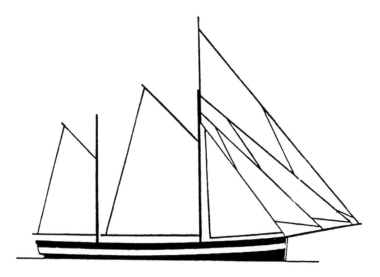

Ketch: *a ketch has two masts. Fore-and-aft rigged. The after-mast (mizzen) is about three-quarters the height of the main and is stepped in front of the tiller.*

River traffic on the Tyne c.1880. Far left, the masts of a large sailing ship moored at Gateshead can just be seen; left, a wherry or possibly a keel; centre, the masted steamship Baldur, registered in Gelfe, discharges timber; right is a brig, probably local.

Index of ships and names